T0393677

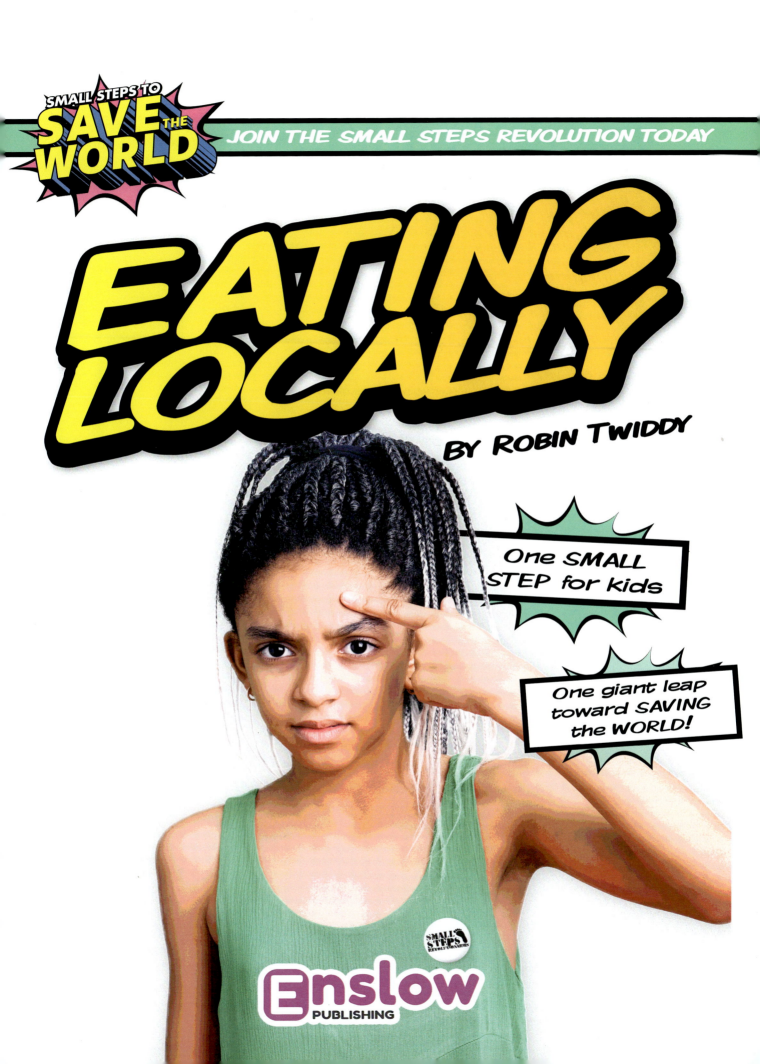

Published in 2023 by Enslow Publishing, LLC
29 East 21st Street, New York, NY 10010

© 2022 Booklife Publishing
This edition is published by arrangement with
Booklife Publishing

Edited by:
Madeline Tyler

Designed by:
Drue Rintoul

All rights reserved. No part of this book may be reproduced in any form without permission in writing from the publisher, except by a reviewer.

Cataloging-in-Publication Data

Names: Twiddy, Robin.
Title: Eating locally / Robin Twiddy.
Description: New York : Enslow Publishing, 2023. | Series: Small steps to save the world | Includes glossary and index.
Identifiers: ISBN 9781978530348 (pbk.) | ISBN 9781978530362 (library bound) | ISBN 9781978530355 (6 pack) | ISBN 9781978530379 (ebook)
Subjects: LCSH: Local foods--Juvenile literature. | Food supply--Juvenile literature. | Sustainable living--Juvenile literature.
Classification: LCC HD9005.T954 2023 | DDC 381'.41--dc23

Manufactured in the United States of America

CPSIA compliance information: Batch #CSENS23: For further information contact Enslow Publishing LLC, New York, New York at 1-800-398-2504

Please visit our website, www.enslowpublishing.com. For a free color catalog of all our high-quality books, call toll free 1-800-398-2504 or fax 1-877-980-4454.

Find us on

PHOTO CREDITS

Images are courtesy of Shutterstock.com. With thanks to Getty Images, Thinkstock Photo and iStockphoto. 4&5 – R.H. Koenig, Kaentian Street, VDWimages, chaiyapruek youprasert, NadyGinzburg, Hung Chung Chih. 6&7 – Daisy Beatrice. 8&9 – Krakenimages.com, Bardocz Peter, Giovanni Cardillo. 10&11 – LanaElcova, Johnathan21, Krakenimages.com, Tatiana Grozetskaya. 12&13 – Tooykrub, Light-Studio, monticello. 14&15 – Monkey Business Images, Krakenimages.com, Julia Sudnitskaya. 16&17 – Arina P Habich, Rawpixel.com, Slatan, Alexey Stiop, ondrejsustik, Stock for you, Andrjuss, Rawpixel.com, Slatan, Naty.M, Ivonne Wierink, Scarc, Iakov Filimonov, Iakov Filimonov, Carolyn Franks, Alex Stemmer, Gorodenkoff, Naty.M, Krakenimages.com. 18&19 – Photographee.eu, Dragon Images, AnnGaysorn. 20&21 – Alena Haurylik, Sorbis, Ministr-84, Krakenimages.com. 22&23 – Krakenimages.com, Alf Ribeiro, Naty.M. 24&25 – Krakenimages.com, Asier Romero, eugenegurkov, Craig Russell, Vasin Hirunwiwatwong, Vadym Zaitsev, Cora Mueller, DarwelShots. 26&27 – Krakenimages.com, fizkes, Rawpixel.com, Monkey Business Images, Mark Janus. 28&29 – Monkey Business Images, Krakenimages.com. 30 – Krakenimages.com.

CONTENTS

PAGE 4	YOU CAN (HELP) SAVE THE WORLD
PAGE 6	Grow Your Knowledge
PAGE 8	Think Globally, Eat Locally
PAGE 10	Carbon Foodprint
PAGE 12	SUPERMARKETS
PAGE 14	Farmers' Markets
PAGE 16	From Farm to Farmers' Market to Fork
PAGE 17	From Farm to Factory to Ship and So On...
PAGE 18	Eating Out
PAGE 20	Fast Food
PAGE 22	Organic
PAGE 24	Grow Your Own
PAGE 26	Becoming a Champion of Change
PAGE 28	Ethical Living
PAGE 30	Manifesto
PAGE 31	Glossary
PAGE 32	Index

Words that look like <u>this</u> are explained in the glossary on page 31.

You can (help) Save the World

The world is in trouble and it needs your help! It needs everyone's help. No one can save the world on their own, but together we can make a change. Our planet is facing many challenges, and lots of these are because of humans. The <u>climate crisis</u> is a big problem. We can see how humans have made it worse by looking at changes in the weather, the oceans, and the air we breathe.

THE SMALL STEPS REVOLUTIONARIES

Formed to save the world, the Small Steps Revolution gains new members every day!

Watch with amazement as the Small Steps Revolutionaries save the world one small step at a time!

Featuring Emilie – the Eating Locally Revolutionary!

These are the Small Steps Revolutionaries. They are changing the world one step at a time. Whether it's being energy efficient or learning how to compost, eating locally or living zero waste, recycling or using water wisely, no problem is too big or too small for this band of heroes. By the time you finish this book, you too will be a member of the Small Steps Revolution. Strap in – it's time to save the world!

Grow Your Knowledge

The first step to becoming a **Small Steps Revolutionary** is growing your knowledge. This means learning as much as you can about the change you want to see. There are lots of ways to grow your knowledge. Here are some places to get started.

Learn from others – do you know anyone who knows a lot about eating locally? Ask them about it.

Visit the library – ask the librarian to help you find books about the environment.

"Knowledge is power – arm yourself!"

"It is time for all of you to leave your comfort zones because it's the uncomfortable things that we do that will be able to save the planet." – Vanessa Nakate

Vanessa Nakate is a Ugandan climate activist.

"Those who do not learn from history are doomed to repeat it!"

Maria Mitchell was an American scientist, astronomer, and librarian who lived in the 1800s.

"Question everything." – Maria Mitchell

Check your local council's website to find out about locally grown and locally sourced food in your area.

Research online – there are lots of great websites about where our food comes from.

Use an online carbon dioxide (CO_2) calculator to find out what your carbon footprint is. (Find out more about your carbon footprint on page 10.)

SMALL STEP: GROW YOUR KNOWLEDGE!

Knowledge is important, but make sure that the information you look at is accurate. A good way to do that is to see who else agrees, writes, or talks about the same information. Has it come from a reliable place or person?

Think Globally, Eat Locally

Hi, I am Emilie, and I am a Small Steps Revolutionary. I eat locally to make a change. That means that the food I buy and eat is grown and sold in the area where I live.

You may be wondering how eating locally is good for the planet. When food is sold a long way away from where it is grown, it needs to travel to be sold – sometimes as far as halfway around the world.

I wonder where my bananas come from...

Different parts of the world have different fruits and vegetables that grow well in those areas.

Carbon Foodprint

CARBON FOOTPRINT

We all have a carbon footprint – this is the amount of carbon dioxide (CO_2) that is released into the atmosphere by the things we do. For example, when you travel in a car, the car releases CO_2 and adds it to the atmosphere, so your carbon footprint grows.

We also add to our carbon footprint in ways that we can't see. When we buy something, all of the CO_2 released when it was made in a factory adds to our carbon footprint. So does all the CO_2 released by the boats, planes, and trucks that carry it from place to place.

Supermarkets

Supermarkets are very <u>convenient</u>. They have almost everything we need in one place. We can buy almost every type of food from all over the world all year round.

Just because something is convenient, it doesn't always mean it's good. When things are very convenient, there is often a hidden <u>cost</u> to the planet. Being a *Small Steps Revolutionary* is about thinking carefully about everything you do — don't be afraid to question things.

We should question how supermarkets keep vegetables and fruits on the shelves that aren't in season.

Many of the foods found on the shelves of supermarkets travel a long way before they make it there. This means lots of CO_2 pollution is made.

Moving food isn't the only way that supermarkets add to their carbon foodprint. Most supermarkets have strict rules about how long fresh food can sit on a shelf. Once food has passed its sell-by date, it can't be sold. Much of this food is given away to charities and used in other ways, but not all of it.

Lots of this food still ends up going to landfill sites when it spoils.

SMALL STEPS:
- QUESTION WHERE YOUR FOOD COMES FROM
- TRY TO BUY FROM SUPERMARKETS THAT GIVE FOOD THEY CAN'T SELL TO CHARITIES

Food waste at landfill sites makes a lot of pollution.

Farmers' Markets

There are other places that we can get our food from. One of the best ways to get food that you know has a low carbon foodprint is going to a farmers' market.

Farmers' markets are places where local farmers sell what they grow. Here are some of the reasons that I go to the farmers' market:

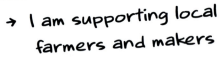

- → I am supporting local farmers and makers
- → Food is freshly picked, in season, and at its most <u>nutritious</u>
- → Buying directly from the farmers means that I can ask questions about what I am buying and how it was grown or raised
- → Less energy is used to move the food from where it was grown or made
- → Lower carbon foodprint

GET CLOSER TO YOUR FOOD

When I go to the farmers' market, I like to talk to the people selling the food. This way I can learn more about the food that I eat, how it is grown, and how it gets to my plate. The people there are as <u>passionate</u> about eating locally as I am.

Because farmers' markets sell food from local farms, you know that it hasn't traveled very far. This means that it has a smaller carbon foodprint and is a great Small Step you can take to make your foodprint smaller.

GROWN LOCALLY

NO PLASTIC PACKAGING

ORGANIC (GO TO PAGE 22 TO READ MORE ABOUT ORGANIC FOOD)

When you buy food at a farmers' market, less packaging is used to wrap it up.

SMALL STEPS: BUY FROM FARMERS' MARKETS WHEN YOU CAN

From Farm to Farmers' Market to Fork

It was just another day at the farmers' market...

There was fruit, vegetables, and all sorts of local produce for sale when...

I wonder where it comes from?

... Kevin, who was shopping with his mom, began to think about all the food there...

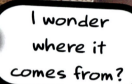

It all begins on a local peach orchard 20 miles (32 km) away.

The peaches are collected.

The peaches are sorted, then chilled to keep them fresh.

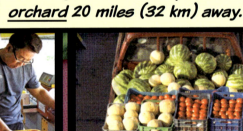

The peaches are taken with other fruits and vegetables to the market.

People set the market stands up, and now the fruit is ready to be sold.

Wow, all that happens right on my doorstep!

From Farm to Factory to Ship and So On...

In a supermarket somewhere in the U.S., Katie and her sister are shopping with their parents.

Wow, there is so much fruit here. I wonder where it all comes from...

Over 6,000 miles (9,650 km) away in Argentina, peaches are grown in an orchard.

The peaches are picked, sorted, washed, and packed for transport.

The peaches are chilled and kept at a low temperature when they are transported by truck...

... then by ship...

... then by truck...

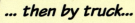

... then finally arrive at the supermarket.

Well, that is a long way!

Not all the fruit in supermarkets travels this far, but lots of it does. Check the labels to see where it was grown.

17

Eating Out

Small Steps Revolutionaries are always thinking about what Small Steps they can take wherever they are. Here are some Small Steps you can take when eating out.

THINK BEFORE YOU CHOOSE

There are all sorts of places where you can eat out. Small Steps Revolutionaries always try to make informed choices – this means learning as much as you can before making a decision.

Here are some questions you can ask yourself:
- Is the restaurant local or is it part of a chain?
- Where do they get their food from?

When a big company owns lots of restaurants that look the same and sell the same food, we call them chain restaurants.

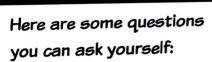

You can find out a lot about a restaurant from its website, but there is no harm in asking the people who work there questions.

When I go to a restaurant, I want to know where they buy their food. Some of the reasons that locally sourced food is better are:
- Locally sourced food has a smaller carbon foodprint
- Locally sourced food is usually fresher — this means that it has more nutrients, is healthier, and usually tastes better
- Because locally sourced food doesn't need to travel very far, nothing needs to be added to keep it fresh for the journey
- It supports local farmers

SMALL STEP: TRY TO CHOOSE LOCAL RESTAURANTS OVER CHAIN RESTAURANTS

Fast Food

When you eat out, it might be at a fast-food restaurant. Fast-food chains have many restaurants that all serve the same food. Usually, they use the same ingredients that come from the same places.

If you get a meal from a restaurant that is part of a chain, it would be almost exactly the same if you got it from the same chain restaurant anywhere else in the same country.

Usually this means that food at a fast-food restaurant has traveled a long way before it is served. So, what is wrong with that? It means that the food has a bigger carbon foodprint and probably uses more <u>chemicals</u> to keep it fresh.

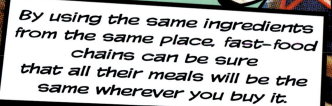

By using the same ingredients from the same place, fast-food chains can be sure that all their meals will be the same wherever you buy it.

20

Fast food is usually made with lower quality ingredients that are higher in fat and cholesterol. These things aren't bad for you on their own, but having too much of them is unhealthy.

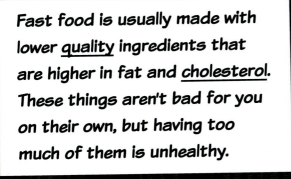

Fast food is convenient. That means that it is fast, easy, and doesn't take much effort to get. It is really handy if you are in a hurry and don't have much time. But "fast food" doesn't have to mean "not local." Can you think of any restaurants near where you live that you could go to instead? Are there any sandwich shops or taco places nearby?

You don't have to stop eating fast food altogether, but if you want to take a Small Step toward eating locally, you can start cutting down on the fast food you eat.

SMALL STEP: CUT DOWN ON FAST FOOD — OR CUT IT OUT COMPLETELY

21

Organic

WHAT DOES ORGANIC MEAN?

One of the main reasons that I eat locally is so that I know how and where my food is grown. I try to find local and organic food. Organic farming is farming that aims to be environmentally sustainable. That means not using anything that would harm the environment.

Remember, a big part of being a Small Steps Revolutionary is knowledge!

WHAT ISN'T ORGANIC?

Who thinks this is a good idea?

Lots of food is not grown in organic ways. It might be grown using chemicals that make it grow faster or bigger, or with chemical <u>pesticides</u>. All of these things can hurt the environment.

22

SUPPORT ORGANIC FARMING

When we support organic farming, we are taking a **Small Step** toward a better, cleaner world. Organic farming creates less waste and pollution and is kinder to animals.

Organic fruits and vegetables can come in funny shapes and all sorts of sizes – but that's just a normal part of nature.

HOW DO I KNOW I AM BUYING ORGANIC?

Always make sure you check the label. Food labels should say if the food was grown in an organic way. If you are buying from a farmers' market, ask the person selling the food – they should know how it was grown. You can even ask at restaurants if their food is organic.

SMALL STEP: BUY ORGANIC

Being a Small Steps Revolutionary means understanding the choices we make.

Grow Your Own

This is my friend Brenda — she is a Composting and Gardening Revolutionary. Her revolution starts with **Small Steps** in the garden.

Emilie always says you should try to eat locally, and there is nothing more local than your own garden! Get your hands dirty in your garden and grow your own food. Growing your own vegetables means that you control exactly how they are grown. You can use organic methods and be sure that your vegetables are completely natural.

Becoming a Champion of Change

Being a Small Steps Revolutionary is more than just taking Small Steps yourself — it also means being a champion of change. We can do this by showing others the steps we are taking and sharing our passion for protecting the planet.

RAISING AWARENESS

There are lots of ways that you can raise awareness as a Small Steps Revolutionary. Some revolutionaries use social media to share their message. <u>Recruit</u> an adult you trust to help you use social media.

You could talk to your teachers to find out where the school cafeteria gets its food from. Maybe they could get their vegetables from local farms instead.

Look for places that you can make a change. Are there any **Small Steps** that could help you and your family eat locally? Talk to your adults to find out if there is a farmers' market near you.

Be the change you want to see.

I got my parents to start buying our fruits and vegetables from a local farmers' market. This apple was grown close to where I live.

Small Steps Revolutionaries are proud to make a change!

Share your successes with the hashtag #smallstepsrevolution

Remember, some people might not have met anyone making the changes you are making, so be nice when you talk about eating locally with them. People are more likely to try to make a change themselves if you are helpful instead of being mean to them – this is the **Small Steps** way!

SMALL STEPS: SHARE YOUR SUCCESSES

27

Ethical Living

Green gardening is only one part of the **Small Steps Revolution**, so what does it mean to be a **Small Steps Revolutionary**? It means living ethically – living the best life you can. To live ethically, you need to think about the effect your actions have on the world around you.

Making the change to eating locally is not easy and won't happen overnight. Remember the golden rule: **Small Steps Lead to Big Change.** Focus on making small changes that you can keep to every day. Every small step will take you closer to eating locally all the time.

THE FIVE Rs

A good way to guide your actions as a *Small Steps Revolutionary* is to live by the Five Rs. They are:

REFUSE – BEFORE YOU BUY SOMETHING, THINK HARD ABOUT WHETHER YOU NEED IT OR NOT. IF YOU DON'T, THEN REFUSE TO BUY OR ACCEPT IT.

REDUCE – SOME THINGS YOU WILL NOT BE ABLE TO REFUSE, BUT YOU CAN USE LESS. THIS WILL MEAN YOU CREATE LESS WASTE.

REUSE – BEFORE YOU THROW SOMETHING AWAY, THINK ABOUT WHETHER THAT THING CAN BE USED AGAIN. ONLY REPLACE SOMETHING IF IT CAN'T BE USED AGAIN.

REPURPOSE – THIS IS ANOTHER WAY OF SAYING UPCYCLE. IF YOU CAN, FIND A NEW WAY TO USE SOMETHING INSTEAD OF THROWING IT AWAY.

RECYCLE – IF YOU CAN'T DO ANY OF THESE THINGS, THEN YOU SHOULD TRY TO RECYCLE. MAKE SURE THAT WHAT YOU PUT INTO YOUR RECYCLING BIN CAN BE RECYCLED BY YOUR LOCAL RECYCLING CENTER.

Manifesto

THE EATING LOCALLY MANIFESTO

- GROW YOUR KNOWLEDGE
- LEARN ABOUT YOUR CARBON FOOTPRINT
- QUESTION WHERE YOUR FOOD COMES FROM
- TRY TO BUY FROM SUPERMARKETS THAT GIVE FOOD THEY CAN'T SELL TO CHARITIES
- BUY FROM FARMERS' MARKETS WHEN YOU CAN
- TRY TO CHOOSE LOCAL RESTAURANTS OVER CHAIN RESTAURANTS
- CUT DOWN ON FAST FOOD — OR CUT IT OUT COMPLETELY
- BUY ORGANIC
- GROW YOUR OWN
- SHARE YOUR SUCCESSES

You are now a full member of the **Small Steps Revolution**. Keep on taking small, sustainable steps, spreading the word and inspiring others to do the same. Together we can and will **Save the World!**

Glossary

ACTIVIST — someone who does things to help raise awareness about a cause

ASTRONOMER — a scientist who studies space, stars, and planets

ATMOSPHERE — the gases that surround the planet

CARBON DIOXIDE — a natural gas that is found in the air that humans breathe out

CHEMICALS — substances that are made or used by scientists

CHOLESTEROL — a substance that is found in the bodies of people and animals

CLIMATE CRISIS — serious problems being caused by changes to the world's weather, caused by humans and the release of greenhouse gases into the environment

CONVENIENT — easily used and easy to get

COST — something that is lost, damaged, or given up in order to achieve or get something

ENVIRONMENT — a natural area in which someone or something lives

IN SEASON — the time during the year that fruits and vegetables are ripe

METHODS — ways of doing something

NUTRITIOUS — having a large amount of minerals and nutrients that the body needs

ORCHARD — a place where people grow fruit trees

PASSIONATE — caring deeply about something

PESTICIDES — chemicals used to stop or kill insects

PRODUCE — fresh fruits and vegetables

QUALITY — how good or bad something is

RAISED — produced and taken care of

RECRUIT — to bring a member into a group

RELIABLE — trusted

RESPONSIBILITY — the need to take on a task or a job that you are trusted to and should do

SOURCED — gotten from a particular place

SPOILS — begins to rot

Index

BRENDA 24

CARBON FOODPRINT 10–11, 13–15, 19, 20

CARBON FOOTPRINT 7, 10–11, 30

CLIMATE CRISIS 4, 6, 9

FACTORIES 4, 10, 17

FARMING 14–17, 19, 22– 23, 27, 30

FAST FOOD 20–21, 30

FRUIT 8, 12, 16–17, 23, 27

GARDENS 24–25, 28

KNOWLEDGE 6–7, 22, 30

MARKETS 12–16, 23, 27, 30

MITCHELL, MARIA 7

NAKATE, VANESSA 6

ORGANIC 15, 22–24, 30

PESTICIDES 22

RESTAURANTS 18–21, 23, 30

SCHOOLS 27

SOCIAL MEDIA 26

SUPERMARKETS 12–13, 17, 30

VEGETABLES 8, 12, 16, 23–25, 27